HOMECOMING

HOMECOMING
-poems-

Hamsa Moily

illustrated by
Kalyani Ganapathy

RUPA

Published by
Rupa Publications India Pvt. Ltd 2014
7/16, Ansari Road, Daryaganj
New Delhi 110002

Sales centres:
Allahabad Bengaluru Chennai
Hyderabad Jaipur Kathmandu
Kolkata Mumbai

Copyright © Hamsa Moily 2014

All rights reserved.
No part of this publication may be reproduced, transmitted,
or stored in a retrieval system, in any form or by any means, electronic, mechanical,
photocopying, recording or otherwise,
without the prior permission of the publisher.

ISBN: 978-81-291-2997-0

First impression 2014

10 9 8 7 6 5 4 3 2 1

The moral right of the author has been asserted.

Printed by Replika Press Pvt. Ltd, India

This book is sold subject to the condition that it shall not, by way of trade or
otherwise, be lent, resold, hired out, or otherwise circulated, without the publisher's
prior consent, in any form of binding or cover other than that in which it is
published.

*To my parents,
who stood by me through my happy and difficult times.
My Pranams to them.*

Contents

Foreword	*ix*
Preface	*xi*
Introduction	*xv*
Introduction to the Artist	*xvii*
An Invocation	1
Krishna	3
The Math of Kalyani	6
In Anticipation	10
Landscapes	14
The Patriot	17
To Hold a Frangipani Flower or Not to Hold	20
Will You Be Mine?	24
Windows	26
A Way of Life	28
Tell Him…	31
After She Returns	35
Change	39
Darkness to Life	42
Death	45
Homecoming	47
The Play of Emotions	50

Monsoons	52
Sun is Shining	56
Tree of Life	59
Inner Way	62
A Diary Dated February 2013	65
Caffeine at the Café	68
The Generous One	70
Dance	74
The Beloved and the Lover	76
It is Not About Seeing, It is About Listening	79
Radha	86
Separation	89
Disentangle	92
Maya	94
These Plastic Buntings	96
Acknowledgements	101

Foreword

The book, *Homecoming*, marks Hamsa Moily's debut as a poet. Sometimes, first works in a particular genre have the endearing quality of innocence, an untouched passion, a directness and simplicity as yet uninfluenced by the predictability of known structures and well-worn theoretical baggage. If there is one reason, above all, why it is a pleasure to read this slim collection of poems it is this.

Hamsa's poetic outpouring is about search. Search not defined in terms of the achievable, but as a fulfilment of the soul. But it is not only about the soul. The body is very much a part of it. A vivid sensuality pervades her poems. The body becomes a metaphor for a deeper yearning, and the intensity of the yearning is such that it bridges the gulf between the sacred and the profane.

The imagery she uses is both direct and subtle, and occasionally unusual. Several poems, like 'Kalyani', 'The Patriot', 'Death', 'Inner Way' and 'Plastic Buntings', to name just a few, show a deep poetic sensibility, and a flow and rhythm that augurs well for her future course as a poet.

But, above all, Hamsa's poems are predominantly a tribute to Krishna. The Blue God is her muse. He is her idiom, her goal, her obsession and her redemption. She pursues him with single-minded devotion, both in His physical form, and in His more elusive incarnation as the promise of deliverance. For her, He symbolizes what needs to be sought, what must be attained, and what can never be held. He is the source of both her joy, and her pain. He is for her the ecstasy of union and the anguish of separation. He remains her grand passion, and even in His absence the only reality that matters. In this sense, Hamsa is the latest avatara of Mira Bai, writing in a different language, but certainly displaying a passion which is of the same kind.

One good thing is that Hamsa's imagery is rooted in the soil. She speaks of the earth and the rain, the banyan tree and the frangipani flower, the waves of the ocean as they embrace the Kerala coast, the colour of Benaras, and the dusk and the dawn of an Indian day. These symbolisms remain her guide even when she broaches a modern subject, away from mythology, or her favourite muse, Krishna. Derivative imagery in poetry is an unforgivable malaise. Hamsa does not make us suffer because of this.

I greatly enjoyed reading Hamsa's collection of poems. I can only pray that she perseveres with the genre and, in doing so, retains her child-like wonder and innocence, her transparent sincerity and the complete absence of guile.

Pavan K. Varma

Preface

This book is a journey, my journey from darkness to life, and hence, autobiographical.

It is my journey as a seeker of life and love; it carries my questions, doubts, memories and some deepest life experiences.

Homecoming has taken birth at a time of in my life, a change that I had been longing for. Being a Bharatanatyam dancer for almost four decades, I had come to a point of no return. The only way to break this was to go spiritual, to break from the limitations of being only a dancer, to becoming an artiste, and much more.

Homecoming was a time for me to embrace old norms, traditions, customs and lifestyles of where I came from, and make a transition to a new life, a new birth. Hence, the title.

This book was not planned. It came to me as a gift from nowhere but I pursued it at a time in my life when I needed it the most. It was as though the world conspired to make this book happen and I accommodated it as an offering and as a salutation.

These poems come from this.

From these poems followed new beginnings. A life that made me look at life with awareness and sensitivity.

These poems contain stories from my life, some old and some new, some containable and some uncontainable.

Some poems came from conversations that I had with people around me, and some came from conversations, which unfolded within the four walls of my room. They are secrets that I have shared.

I thought poetry only happened to other people; to those who had the ability to play with words, those with a voracious vocabulary, sincere and sacred. I thought I came with none of these but just a dance form that carried me till here.

These poems happened to me when I was ready to take on the world, a hopeful world.

These poems are made of these, of optimism.

Through this journey of poems, I discovered spaces familiar and unfamiliar.

This book is contemporary, which has grown from old traditions.

Many things changed in my life during the writing of this book. Life has never been the same for me since then.

It has been challenging no doubt but, at the same time, cleansing, healing, a flowering of my own being.

This book is about many things. It's about love that is conditional and unconditional. It energized me existentially.

I have spent much of my life wanting to know, consciously and subconsciously, about the mysteries of life. Through these poems, I have tried to address some of the mysteries which have intrigued me all my life, some questions with answers and some left as questions and more questions.

Though I can say it is the subconscious that has brought me here, I hope I have conveyed this in my poems.

Poetry came to me in silence and at a time when I was seeking for silence and more silence. Through this silence of my life unravelled the mysteries of life. This unravelling brought clarity within me and therefore in my poems.

These poems are of seeking and a search for more in life.

My sincere thanks to Rupa Publications for their openness and keen attention to making this book happen.

I am grateful to all those who held these poems as close to their heart as I have.

I am grateful, above all, to my Guru, Sadhguru Jaggi Vasudev, who made me see life through these poems, which contain within them a rhythm. The same rhythm which carries with it a song of devotion, a song of silence which is in nothingness. This book is about a journey, my journey of life. It is based on my conversation from within and with-out therefore, I become the narrator.

These poems come from this.

Introduction

I met Hamsa almost two decades ago and have seen this petite and graceful girl blossom into a fine individual. A sensitive person, she radiates an inner beauty that makes her personality both mysterious and appealing. Her unassuming and friendly nature has endeared her to many.

When we started working together, I saw a practical side to her that I did not know existed. When I choreograph any item, I do not put down the notes on paper, just assuming I would not forget whatever ideas I've strung together. If I do forget, I just attempt to recreate it from the beginning. Hamsa, however, really impressed me as she not only has the choreography ideas on paper but also all the schedules for rehearsals neatly typed out. I must admit that I now have started jotting down my ideas but my notes are no way as meticulous as those of Hamsa!

Her insightful portrayal of Radha in *Geeta Govind* was a moving experience, creating an unforgettable rasaanubhaava for the audience.

She is a perfectionist. Whether it is dance, theatre or writing, she is never fully satisfied until her work turns out just the way she imagined it.

These poems reflect her deep sensitivity, something integral to who Hamsa is.

Minal Prabhu

Introduction to the Artist

'With folded palms I bow…' begins this collection of meditative and deeply personal poems. A salutation to Shiva. '…Let there be a war, within and without'.

The poet has danced herself to place where the delicate balance of being and non-being leaves her and us, her readers, suspended, vulnerable and longing. We share her moments of ecstasy and loss as she ponders on these inescapable truths.

Until the last poem of the collection, which suddenly brings us back to modern reality where 'plastic' is ever-present, the reader is taken on a journey in a timeless zone.

We are one with the infinite sensuality of Krishna and Radha. One with the sap of life. Aloneness is as pervasive as is the feeling of being connected, fused like a lover to the source of all things, material and immaterial.

Though the poems are filled with vivid colour and images—a miniature painting come alive—the poet urges one to not trust what one sees but rather listen to sounds and to the silence between the sounds. Then one can begin to slowly sway to barely perceptible whispers. And finally to dance, lost and found and lost again.

There is nothing to hold. One can only keep listening.

Adam Shapiro★

★is a grower of trees. He also makes paintings. He has known the poet for many years.

An Invocation

With folded palms
I bow to the Presence
within...
There is silence within.

I meditate whilst
I keep to the rhythm
of the fundamental Truth.
Feel, seek,
yearn, die—
breathlessly,
for the Ultimate.

To be
is to exist, is to be beside the Truth.
To be, when I am nothing.
To be, when I am nowhere.
To be, when I am there.
Eyes close to set
the body afloat.

Let there be a war,
within and without,
I am taking a deep breath
to drink the Truthfulness.
Let there be darkness,
the light always conquers.
So, I explore and travel...

As I walked and fumbled
and walked and fell
at the foothills
of the seven
white mountains,
stillness surrounded me.
Stillness...
that which is, is Shiva,
that which is not, is Shiva.

Krishna

A dark blue
clear and cold night,
with countless bright stars
and a full moon
that lights up
the earth.

Black mountains,
with deers making their
way back into the forest.
Valleys flow,
to join
the ocean.

Crickets chirp
loud, to wake up
the fireflies.
The fireflies
light up
the shrubs.

In silence,

on a flowerbed,
she sits,
with half-opened eyes,
her splendid skirt in red
encircles her.
She is Radha.
Closest to her,
is her beloved Krishna, the dark God.
Entwined unto each other.
Radha bares her naked breast,
with bangles made of
pearls on her wrists.

Krishna
beholds her
and holds her slender waist, delicately.
He sits,
vibrantly in his
turmeric-coloured garment
with a stole that glides
along as a stream,
and a turban
that matches Radha's splendid skirt in red.

Radha,
bejewelled
from head to toe
for her Beloved.
She sits gracefully…
for her Beloved

as He paints
her naked breast.

Behind her
sits her husband
with a fortune smile,
he watches,
the love play of
Krishna and Radha.

The Math of Kalyani

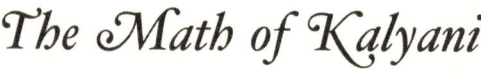

She dances
while she walks.

Kalyani,
namesake
of my mother's mother.
A light. A light
into my life, in a red blanket,
wrapped up
warmly.
Her warmth follows me,
long after she
has left her room in my kutiram.
Escapes swiftly
even before I call
out to her, my Kalyani,
namesake
of my mother's mother,
who left my mother when she was all of four.
Four was my age, when I got initiated to dance.
Four is the date,
when K left me... his kidneys gave way to death.

Fourteen is the date,
while I wept when,
I grew into a woman yet not ready.
Thirty-one years ago,
three and one adding up to four.

Four is the number, I seek to forget but
now I write four,
the word 'four' I forgot, yet not the digit four.

Kalyani,
seventeen months old, wrapped up in a red blanket,
warmly...
one adding up to seven
equals eight.
Eight, multiple of four.

Kalyani,
A light, a light in my life and Swastika, the auspicious four.
Born on one and seven, adding up to eight, multiple of four.
Swastika, made of vermilion.
Kalyani,
she sat,
in gratitude, plainly and simply
in my old home,
bowing to the Yantra
of Shakti.
Shakti has her

third eye
adorn the vermilion today.

Kalyani danced,
her Truth in gratitude, plainly and simply,
free and carefully,

Kalyani,
in my old home.
My new home,
spreads
a rangoli of the son of Shiva,
in purity and in white on grey granite.

Kalyani,
dances in her yellow skirt,
joyously.

Swastika,
the number four,

a cycle of time, time of Kalyani and my time,
thus, the cycle and thus a revolving sun and thus infinity,
Kalyani,
namesake,
of my mother's mother.
Kalyani, in my life,
Swastika
and the auspicious four.
Born on one and seven,

adding up to eight,
multiple of four.

In Anticipation

Birds fly,
back to their nests,
their day's work
has come to an end.
The dark clouds
are in slow motion.
The full moon
has hidden behind them.

The most beauteous place
is lit up today, with
thousands of oil lamps.
Each wick is smeared,
with camphor.
This is where
He would walk in tonight.

I am amongst the others
but it is not me.
His grace has touched me.

With my head up
in pride,
I walk out of here.
The full moon has
showed up finally,
as the dark clouds
make way.

He drives past me
majestically.
I have been
longing to see Him.
I have waited
from morning till night,
for days and nights,
for this night of union.

Alas! He has walked
past me,
without a glance
and faded away
from my eyes.
Not even a glimpse at me.
'Is this what you are?
Or is it the circus of my mind?' I walked away
in silence,
with a hope of
meeting Him
at midnight.

The dark clouds
are in slow motion.
The full moon
has hidden behind them
once again.

Darkness all around
and within me.
Only a glance
at me,
for a moment,
I desire.

Alas! I slept through it all...
while I waited.
He came and left.
Why this unfair
behaviour?

But I dreamt of Him,
in my sleep.
He spoke to me,
in my sleep.
He sat with me,
in my sleep.

He sent me a message,
in my sleep
that He would arrive,
in my city
after seven long days.

'You will arrive...
won't you?
Give me a glance...
won't you?'

Landscapes

A landscape of
an earthen pot filled with water
with an earthen cup beside it,
placed in the corner of a room.
Yellow-mustard wall paint, painted
in the background of a wall.
A young maiden
in red salwar-kameez
lazily lies down on a charpai
with eyes half-open.
A red bindi made of vermillion
adorns her forehead
and sindoor smeared in the parting
of her hair.
Alta painted on her feet and palms.
A black quilt with red floral embroidery
thrown on the mattress, the rest of it,
on the floor.

A landscape of
an Indian bride sits pretty
in her red gharara.

With a grandly embroidered
chiffon dupatta, loosely wrapped around
her head and covering her chest and arms.
Metal of gold glitters
on top of her head.
Her tiny wrist adorns a thick bracelet
made of teak with
gold embellishments.
Her eyes look eager at the
news of her bridegroom.

A landscape of
three maids, surround
the young maiden, who carefully
place her on a swing.
Her bare feet barely
touch the ground,
her ankles bear anklets
of silver metal.
Veils from Banaras in black and red
cover their heads.
A palace in white with a fort
in the background.
The young maiden is
preparing for her wedding.

A landscape of
men and women gather outside
the fort of the palace.
Children gather gleefully

around a wise old man,
who is narrating stories of centuries old.
A woman draped in a veil of red organza,
is seated, waiting for the fabrics
inside the boiling pots
to catch the dyes made of vegetables.
An urli with red hibiscus
is placed, filled with water
on the ground.
In the background, two women
decorate the doorway
with orange marigold flowers.

The Patriot

You are a patriot,
when you allow
yourself to migrate
to lands
unfamiliar.

Either you are a patriot
or you are not.
It is about being,
black
and white.

You are a patriot,
when you swallow
beauty
down your
muscles.

You are a patriot,
when you watch
infants beside their
mothers.
It beckons you.

You are a patriot,
when workers who get
daily wages
from their vendors,
teach you humility.

You are a patriot,
when you pay salutations
to people, who come in
contact
with your eyes.

You are a patriot,
when you go hunting
for hand-crafted items
from all over the world,
remarkable and proper.

You are a patriot,
when you strive
for the best.
At every moment
and every breath.

You are a patriot,
when your garden
bears a variety
of hibiscus
and betel nut trees.

You are a patriot,
when you spend
your money
on hand-woven
khadi and ahimsa fabric.

You are a patriot,
when your mobile phone
has numbers of
people from different
religion, caste and creed.

You are a patriot,
when a freefall
engulfs you
to encounter
the Enlightened,
Only if you are black and white.

To Hold a Frangipani Flower or Not to Hold

In my garden this lone tree grows.
Flowers sprout in bunches and bunches
and blossom like how rain poured,
on that day, when I moved into
my home, made of earth
and only earth.

This tree speaks of that evening,
that evening, when it rained and poured and poured.
This tree is of that evening.
The flower speaks of that evening
when music of the flute
brought tears like rain.
The flower is of that evening.

She distracts me,
this flower, from my lover who now lives…
seven seas away
away from me and
away from my frangipani bunches of flowers,
These temple flowers.

A frangipani flower is a
wine of desire, of hundred desires.
Her fragrance, takes me away from my lover
but makes me his,
who now lives...seven seas away.

The depth of the sea, is what I see...
when I look at a flower
of a temple tree.
The petals are not petals,
they are the many suns
that have been rising and setting
through eons...
dawns and dusks, many cycles of them.

They do not sell this flower in the market place...
you know that,
don't you?
It grows in your garden,
a garden where
friends dance and sing songs,
intoxicated by the smell
of this flower, the frangipani flower.

To not hold her...
this flower, the frangipani flower,
is to search...
on a beach sand,
for shells....
You do not search for them,

you walk on the beach sand
and find them
beside your bare feet...
and hold them
and love them
and leave them
right there, where they belong.

To not hold her
this flower, the frangipani flower,
is to end before it can start...
a love story
that is endless, ruthless
and unforgiving.
This is a love story,
do not go by any other,
it is a silent one
and the only one.

Oh my love!
Are you the flower?
This frangipani one?
Or are you in disguise?
You are the torturous one....
who now lives...
seven seas away.

Drink the fragrance
of this flower, the frangipani flower...
bring him to you,

who lives seven seas away
make him yours
and yours alone.

Then when he sits beside you,
talk about her, the frangipani flower,
who now lives,
as a lone tree in bunches and bunches,
in my home, made of earth
and only earth.

Will You Be Mine?

Will you be mine
and mine alone?
A dream I had
Of you
kissing me.
And I thought...
you do not have time for me.
You are deceptive...
the deceptive one.

On a Thursday morning,
a very early one,
you held me by my arm,
ruthlessly,
and said to me...
in a tender tone,
'you are mine and mine alone.'

I blushed...
and the one standing alone
away from you and me,
saw us whisper
secrets of love and lust.

Tomorrow,
will you come again?
And touch my arm
and caress it?
Holding me...is a far off dream.

Will you come tomorrow?

You did,
in a dream...
on a Thursday morning,
a very early one.

You held me by my palm,
and made me write...
Words...
Words that spoke of love and lust,
Sitting beside me...in the dark of the morning
before dawn.

You wrote...with my palm,
'You are mine
and mine alone.
Do not go by people's
madness,
be with me.' Will you be mine?
I ask again,
Will you be mine?

Windows

Outside my windows in the south,
is a Mahogany tree, lush
with green leaves,
ably strong.
Outside my windows,
Mahogany, moving...as the wind blows subtly.
Memories of the colours
of a peacock feather
that He wore.

Outside my windows in the east,
shades of mustard, red and white
from a garden of hibiscus plants.
Memories of an artiste, whose birth centenary
we now celebrate at a gallery.

Outside my windows in the west,
women dressed in saris,
cycle joyously and sturdily
on tar roads.
Passing by children gleefully,
watch the full moon
under a banyan tree.
Memories of the raasleela
of Krishna in the spring.

Outside my windows in the north,
stands my home,
whitewashed.
Memories of a room with a view of the sea,
waves roaring in the
stillness of the night.
Birds chirp from their nests,
am listening to a song.

A Way of Life

Parks made of lush green

gardens in excess.

Children only between the age

of one to five are allowed.

Simply, watch these beautiful beings

and their games.

Parents, maids,

seesaw, monkey-bar, merry-go-round

swing or slide...are prohibited.

Competition

will be the rule of the day,

only in sports

and creative writing

for children of all ages.

Rural India will till

agricultural land.

Bicycles and private jets

will be their mode of transport.

Daily newspapers will

carry pages and pages of art

and works of artists

will be on display.

People in cities will live

in glass houses.

Transparent windows without grills.

With fruit and

vegetable

market inside.

A river at every kilometre.

Fish and crocodiles will

swim in plenty.

And music every moment,

either someone humming or

from the radio.
Countries without borders.

Countries with respective languages.

And

absolutely,

no need for

talks on peace processes.

This list is endless.

Tell Him...

Tell Him…

I will not go to my husband's home.

I will stay here in a dark room.

I will be with my eyes closed.

Until He arrives.

The moon is yet to set.

In the forest the elephants have disappeared.

I watch an elephant carrying a man,

in my big city.

Tell Him…

only when He arrives, will

the moon set.

Only when He arrives, will the elephants

appear again in the forest.

Tell Him...

Send Him a note saying,

I am lost...

without Him.

I saw Him last night,

far away from me.

He walked past several others

without turning back to look at me

without a note for me,

while He walked past several others.

The mirror, in front of it, I sat

to dress up for Him, for I know that

He will arrive

tonight.

I sat down

to highlight my eyes with kohl...

for Him,

in front of the mirror.

The mirror reflects Him,

the truth revealed

and the colour I become of His.

His eyes become mine.

He is present, He is omnipresent.

The arrow has pierced my heart
and the cupid begins his game.
Let the game begin...

He is present, He is omnipresent.

I bare my chest and dare to bare,

the arrows pierce my heart,

an arrow made of mango flowers

and another flowers from a raintree.

Both bringing me close, closer to death.

There is a way to awaken me

from my unconscious state

to the subconscious.

The latter delivers me to Him.

While He walked past several others,

He picks my subconscious,

and walks away, far away

and takes me to His abode,

where I live now.

The city was lit up today,

With a strange colour, they said

When He arrived…

After She Returns

It is not easy to

break away from the past.

I know that.

Even if I leave it,

there is somebody

who will

bring it back

to me.

She returned,

treading with

her head held high,

picked up the pieces

from where she had left,

put them together

to reinvent life.

The dark God, never met her again

after He left Vrindavan...so they say. He did

within her, He lived

as her only companion.

It is not easy to

break away from the past.

I know that.

So, I detach myself

from all ties.

I am insane to do this...

But that is the way

The only way.

At another place,

away from

the past,

she and her Beloved

secretly met,

at another place.

He was not her cowherd anymore,

He was Shri Krishna.

This is where they met...

birds chirped,

in the bower.

He made her bed neatly and meticulously.

In the wild, He handpicked flowers

which were scented.

Decorated the bed

with those flowers.

Sprayed rose water

on the bed.

He took her by the wrist

gently and tenderly,

inviting her

to be seated

on this bed.

Radha and her Beloved,

secretly met,

at another place.

He was not her cowherd anymore,

He was Shri Krishna.

Change

In severe winter,
leaves fall away,
giving way
to fresh young
leaves in
parrot-green.
Parrots with red beaks
settle
on the tree.

In my neighbourhood,
children's voices
are in gay abundance,
echoing into my home.
Childhood
is playful
and continuous.

Children,
waiting in a queue
with empty plates
for free lunch

and free education.
How did we
move into this
reality?

Change is the order.
A convict
surrenders.
Surrender is resurrection.
Surrender is reverence.

Elephants,
do not destroy elephants.
Mankind has become
contradictory.

Humans
break humans
to pieces.
Humans blindfold
humans.

There are only a
few pieces of
clothing in my wardrobe
that are required
for survival.
A fetish for footwear
is simply not essential.

Paw marks of leopards
inside concrete homes.
We have taken possession
of their homes.
It is time to give way
to animal farms.

Astronauts
have gone to the ancient
moon
to find craters.
Dig deep.
There is enough
in this lifetime
to find oneself.

The masculine
and the feminine
are both within.
It is existential.
The within
mirrors the with-out.

Darkness to Life

A girl, all of fourteen,
can come alive
only after
surpassing hurdles,
those endless hurdles.

An adult-child
she is.
January is her name.
January wore spectacles
which gave her access,
to people's way of life.
It was her secret world.

Every time she
put a step forward,
she was pulled down
by a thousand steps.
She learnt that,
people projected
their fears on to her.

For every truth she spoke,
she was battered.
January,
The unfortunate one.
But she gave her life
for people.
January,
The compassionate one.

People saw her
as a child.
January,
kept her adulthood alive
to learn.

'You are the pure one,' a saint,
once said to her.

Exhausted, one day,
she knelt down
with her arms,
embracing her knees,
face down...
a world
of people
living in darkness
was revealed to her.
The ordinary people.

When January
was all of forty-one,
she was whisked away
by an eagle.
She disappeared, far away,
away from
her family,
her friends,
her lover.
There she found life,
her bright life.

Death

Rebirth in
different lifetimes.
Lifetimes with death.
It is burdensome.

It is not the deaths
we fear,
it is the rebirths
we fear.

A new life is the
new leaf.
Only if
we overcome,
lifetimes of death.

The rivers
of India
are reminders of death.
The river swallows
death.

Those who sacrifice life,
float into death.
Fire dissolves
the body into ashes.
Ashes dissolve
into the river.

Feel it,
you will know,
the many deaths
that the river
carries.

See your face,
in this river.
You will not
escape death.

Death is the truth.
There is life.
There is death.
Two sides of a coin.

Homecoming

You are brought into
the existence by Him.
This is homecoming.
The womb becomes your passage
to do His work in this world.

This is homecoming,
when you know
that you are looked after.
He kneads you,
puts you on the potter's wheel.
His hands take the shape
of you.

This is homecoming,
when you wake up
to see sunshine
and its shadow,
in your wakefulness
from bed.

This is homecoming
when you perceive...
wherever you are,
however you are,
whatever you do,
you know,
it is His work,
24/7, 365 days a year,
ethereally. This is homecoming,
when He makes you
aware of the truth.
The falseness doesn't
stick to you anymore.
Memories fade out...
a freshness ascends
and falls in your lap.
Suddenly one day,
all you see is newness.

This is homecoming,
when you arrive at
every space which is
custom-made for you.
Fears, doubts, suspicion,
go out through
a window.
More windows
open out
every moment.
These moments

are pure and they
do not recur.

This is homecoming.
When He tends to you,
then picks you.
Everything,
everything is predestined.
You feel it is your success but
It is Him,
making you, sculpting you.
His design works through you.

You become sensitive
and strong
because
He lives within you.
He chooses you to become
an instrument for change.

The Play of Emotions

You promised me never
to remind me about,
the dark old days.
But you brought them back
today,
when all I experienced was fantastical.
Why this play of emotions?

It is an early evening,
I am content without you today,
when you decide to disrupt me,
with thoughts of you.
Why this play of emotions?

My lover whispers,
sweet nothings into my ears.
But it so happened that yesterday,
you reminded me of all the stories of misunderstanding,
between him and me.
Why this play of emotions?

Blue is his favorite colour.

But I see you wear them
in grandeur.
I am confused.
Why this play of emotions?

People with masks on,
communicate with me.
I have taken mine off,
to be with you.
But you repeatedly,
send me to those who fake it.
Why this play of emotions?

I recall, those who come from
your country, are people who live
with smiles.
But somebody there
robbed me off my possessions.
You show me a picture of untruth.
Why this play of emotions?

It always rains
when you arrive.
It's intending to rain today,
but I see no sign of you.
Why this play of emotions?

Monsoons

The weather

forecast indicates,

that there will

be rain.

The wind also carries the message

that the rain is soon to follow.

I wait in traffic, huge trucks

surround me

and on either side

trees.

I see first drops

of rain fall

on these trees.

Become rain

in my country.

Rain…

But not your fury.

The rising water

of the Ganga

is wild and violent.

Uttarkashi

collapses.

Become rain

in my country.

Rain…

But not your fury.

River Tehsil

has submerged.

my home, a humble home

in the village.

My tree with curry leaves

has fallen into

the angry,

River Tehsil

I stand alone.

In front of me

the earth has

split open.

The road to

Govindghat

is remote.

Two women,

ride a scooter

on a waterlogged

street of Lucknow.

They have not seen her

fury yet.

The fury of rain!

The ocean

has uprooted

my family.

The coconut trees

are washed away.

Our livelihood

washed away.

Become rain

in my country.

Rain...

But not your fury.

Sun is Shining

The ferryman takes
me across,
River Krishna.
The vast blue sky,
accompanies me
through
my journey.
The sun is shining.
My eyes long
to see the shore.

The rocky
terrain
is full of thorns.
I am told
one must
walk barefoot
here.
While
the sun is shining,
pain is of no
significance.

My home is on fire.
But there is no need
to be dejected.
The sun is shining
at another home.

The sun is shining,
while a sculptor
hurts his fingers
while sculpting.
The sculpture
is complete
only after suffering.

There is news of him visiting me today...
here in Banaras.
The city has
a golden glow.
The sun is shining
on the Ganga river.
The people
in the ghats
bathe
themselves,
with warmth.

Behold the sun
in your eyes.
The mystic
lives in there.

Homecoming ~ 57

And do close
your eyes when
the eclipse dances
in there.
The dance
is eternal.
But you are mortal.

Break the cycle,
Break the rhythm,
Break the myths,
Break yourself,
Break death.
Here is an opportunity,
for liberation.

Tree of Life

That tree of life
is made of ink
from vegetable dyes
with hunger, toil and
sweat.

This tree of life
is about life,
about the paths
that cross and
about new paths that
take on different roles.

The red earth is cultivated,
and the seed is sown.
This is so in life…
The 'sacred' seed is the source
of life.
It is His presence.
The seed anchors itself
deeply into the soil.
So does His presence
He persists.

The roots take on
the form of
the trunk.
The branches shoot
out of the trunk.
And life
grows because of His presence.

The trunk now
maps the
destination of the tree.
This is so in life…
His presence maps our destination
and life reaches its ultimate nature.

Branches give rise to
more branches.
Life is about stories.
Stories within stories.
This is an organized process.

Buds swell up for flowering.
And then there is flowering.
Every life in flesh and bone
goes through the winding paths.
For this,
He gives His life and more.

It is the waiting
which makes the tree

abundant with leaves and flowers.
It is the waiting that makes you abundant with
flowering and colour.

The bees from the flowers
buzz songs of new birth.
The pollination from the bees and the wind
gives birth to a new life.
So does life, every moment
always in search of a new life.
This is the beginning.

Inner Way

Young butterflies flutter from
one place to another,
in millions as migrants,
to make a journey.
Plain yellow butterflies
pass by me.
I am told…that I am
few steps closer to Him.

Children walk to
school.
On their way
they stop on the far side of me,
excited to greet Him.
I stand along with them
to greet Him…
I am told…I am
few steps closer to Him.

River Tungabhadra flows swiftly,
churning the boatman.

I sit and watch the river water
filling up the boat.
As my hands touch the river lightly,
a call from a monk on my telephone,
said, 'He has arrived.'
I am told…I am
few steps closer to Him.

The sky heavy with dark clouds,
brings down pouring rain.
I rise from sleep as the wind,
blows my hair onto my face.
His stole hangs free on one side
of the wall near the window sill.
I embrace it as
thunder and lightning cross each other.
I am told…I am few
steps closer to Him.

My lover and I stay indoors to share
mysteries of a world,
where only mystics go.
Bed disheveled,
I step away from my lover
to dress up.
In front of me
is a mirror…there,
I find Him in a forest.
I am told… I am few
steps closer to Him.

Rocks in intimate union,
reflect an energy that is fiery.
A heavy sky,
with schoolchildren,
the boatman, my lover and I,
gather together on the beach.
Ahead is the vast ocean.
'It is Him here'...I call out insanely...
'He, who has always been with me!,
He, who has always been with me!'

A Diary Dated February 2013

A girl child in my life,
on a Thursday morning.

We knelt down writing about our travels,
she in her black glossy diary and I in my spiral bound one.

Our travels matched.

She demanded a long list
from me
but I followed her thoughts.

Her supple thoughts
which were also mine.

The best places in the world we chose
and to all parts of India.

We pulled out a map of India
and travelled with our pens.

We went to the mountains
of Kailash
and then came down to the sea,
the best of Indian sea
The Arabian Sea.

All this sitting on an Afghan carpet
my father brought home
from a Sunday flea market.

What happened today?
What happened today?
We went to see the crafts of Bastar...
She and I went to Bastar
on a red Afghan carpet.
The wooden crocodiles swam below us
and as we slowly descended,
pretty wooden dolls sat there
watching the
crocodiles swim beside them...
And baskets of various fabric and yards and yards of saris,
she draped herself with.

We left the saris and the crocodiles and the rest of all
to go to another land
in India.
A land which dated back
to the 13th century,
where poets were
Enlightened.

Enlightened they were.
Their poetry raw
but flowed like a river.
They were of a different kind.
A kind you don't find
these days.
Their eyes sparkled
like their ear lobes
which were adorned with diamond-
studded stones.
Their fingers as soft
as lotus petals.
Their souls
as white
as the lotus petals.

A diary dated February 2013

Caffeine at the Café

As I strolled from the café
into a shop
and on to the threshold of another shop,
I saw him at a distance,
speaking
with a woman.
I called out to him
in a whisper
and walked away
in apprehension.

I looked at the clothes…
hung
on the rack and
out of habit but disinterested.
I walked out of the shop,
into the other shop.
Standing on the threshold,
I saw him again at a distance,
busy at work and
caressing the dress…
hung

on the rack.
I walked away
into the same café.

As I sat on a chair, hungry,
looking at the temple tree...
through a window
and drunk on cappuccino,
he walked
to my table.
He came forward
gently and softly...
whispered a kiss on my cheek
and then the other
in precision.

When I only saw the Divine
and only the Divine...
Pure and Truth.
Nothing
but the Divine.

The Generous One

The Generous One

And the sensuous one

you are.

Your fingers

that speak of lifetimes,

are soft, as soft

as a muslin cloth.

You are a sufi,

the best one

I have known

from lifetimes, I have treaded.

The generous one

you are.

A phone call, on

one silent night...

when the universe conspired.

Your voice beside me

all night till dawn.

Many wakeful nights

we spoke on our cell phones

with numbers

that dialed

09u72519632
and

0m639201739

for months.

Those nights

turned into

days of phone calls

that dialed

09u72519632

and

0m639201739...

for months on end.

We spoke of paths

we walked

and travelled

in our lifetimes.

Generous...

I call you because you were

there

when all

left

me

without

a word...

Dance

Dance is the
only deepest
expression.
Dance of life
comes from
a river,
a stream.

Dance is pure
and untouched.
It touches the most
sacred part of you.
It is Divine.
It comes from
within.

Dance comes
from nature.
The wind blows
only for the trees.
Just like how the breath
keeps the beat
for you.

Dance is the only
way...
to welcome
life.
It is the only purpose
of life.

Dance is,
about your toes,
your feet,
your fingers,
your palms,
your arms,
your heart.

Dance is,
about you and you alone.
It lives
in your blood,
in your veins
and
in your bones.

Dance has no religion,
no community,
no creed.
Dance has flight,
dance is grounded,
dance is music.
Dance is everywhere.

The Beloved and the Lover

The Beloved and
the lover I love.
The Beloved goes beyond
the lover, though the lover is
loved and worshipped.

The lover is jealous
about the Beloved,
who lives within me.
The Beloved cannot be reached,
unless you become His.

Thoughts together of
the Beloved and the lover
is a strange feeling.

Thoughts about
the lover is a result of
my conditioned mind.
Or am I merely a puppet
in the hands of the Beloved?

The only way is to be
in the game with
the Beloved.
The lover and I become
secondary.

The lover and I
are contenders in an arena.
But the Beloved controls
and plays it His way.

I hold within me,
the Beloved and the lover.
I get the pain,
the lover gets pleasure.

What is it that makes
the relation between
the Beloved and me...
continuous
and overwhelming?

The Beloved is longed
for, every single moment...
day and night.
The lover comes in
and goes away in my memory.

The loner that I am,
longs for a lover too.

I ask the Beloved...
what is this dichotomy?
Do reveal the secret?

'It has taken my life
to trust you...
my Beloved.
Your skillfully engineered
ways have made me sleek.' It is at the time
of mindlessness,
that the Beloved captured me.
And thus, He captivates...
The lover sits beside.
I ask the Beloved,
Then why does the lover
entice me?

My lover and I sit down
over a conversation.
Our eyes speak more than words...
'Will you embrace me?'
the Beloved interrupts.

It is Not About Seeing,
It is About Listening

It is Not About Seeing,

It is About Listening.

Seeing is believing they say,

I say, it is about listening.

The energy spreads…

it is all connected.

From the sound of people,

listen carefully.

There is rejoicing in

the air.

Seeing is believing they say,

I say, it is about listening.

When you pause...

in moments,

the nature marries you.

You can hear

the stillness.

It is palpable.

Seeing is believing they say,

I say, it is about listening.

When I listen to the radio,

between the tunes of a song,

the water flows.

There is a river nearby...!

Pick up those tunes and celebrate the river.

Seeing is believing they say,

I say, it is about listening.

The blue flowers from

the Jacaranda tree

is a temptress.

When the wind blows,

the sound of it overtakes…

it becomes lustrous.

Seeing is believing they say,

I say, it is about listening.

The nothingness

is heard only,

only because of the sound.

The sound that is given

to you,

you cannot take it by force.

Seeing is believing they say,

I say, it is about listening.

In the midst of chaos,

birds chirp mirroring

the city.

Listen to them carefully...

they will

transform you.

Seeing is believing they say,

I say, it is about listening.

There is a saying, 'actions speak

louder than words.'

The action is a response

from what you get

between

every word.

Seeing is believing they say,

I say, it is about listening.

If you listen to the rhythm

of this city,

you will know about

the kind of people who live here.

You need to be brave

to hear the sounds of this world.

Seeing is believing they say,

I say, it is about listening.

The craftsmanship of a chest of drawers

is physical.

But the sound of his work,

is silent in nature.

You appreciate the silence of his work.

It will make you joyous.

Seeing is believing they say,

I say, it is about listening.

You perfect a dance,

not from songs,

but from that which is soundless.

It is an endless struggle

but you finally get it right.

Seeing is believing they say,

I say, it is about listening.

You can hear the words

but they are best heard,

when you here the breath

in between words.

An artiste said to me,

that her work is to find the music

between notes.

A decade has gone by.

Has she found the notes?

I have heard it...in my very being.

Radha

Radha breaks out of
all ties,
to be with her cowherd.

A sheer veil over her head,
hidden, Radha steps out,
on a still night,
to be with her cowherd.

She awaits in the green fields,
from dusk to dawn,
for her cowherd to arrive,
Radha, the stubborn lover.

'You give me your flute…
and in return take my veil,'
she invites her cowherd.
'Let me merge into you…
and you into me…Kanha,'
longs Radha.

She accuses,
her cowherd of loving
and lusting after the
womenfolk,
whom she resents.
Daringly, Radha laments to the world…
'The Raasleela was only played with me and me alone.'

She displays her ceremonial costume.
A chest of drawers with jewels is
waiting, to be worn at her marriage
with her cowherd.
The nose ring on her shines bright, blinding her.
Tears run down her cheeks,
The cowherd has not appeared today.
'I am mad about you, don't you see?' she questions.

'The cowherd has walked away
selfishly…
without taking me
with Him…
why so stone-hearted

have you become?
Are you going back to your wedded wife tonight?
Can't you see I am broken?
Kanha.'
Radha, the fair-complexioned one argues.

She waits for him
in a garden with creepers
of white jasmine.
The flowers bloom in the night
when the cowherd meets Radha.
'You are my companion...
Or will you forget me...
meet me again, won't you?
or would you leave me?'
Radha urges Him.

'Come away from the land where evil descends
Or come back Kanha after you defeat your evil uncle.'
Radha awaits...
while Krishna departs for the Kurukshetra war.
He never returned...

Separation

After a long separation
He flew down to be with me.
Alas! He departs...
But promises to come back.
I feel a sense of loss
after He has gone.
Dear friend,
What is this mischief all about?
Tell Him to come and fetch me.

My heart overflows,
when I think of Him.
But
alas! He disappoints me...
I look around in
search of Him.
Dear friend,
Call Him and summon Him
Or take me where He lives.

I lie down with my hair
open to the fumes of charcoal.

My drunken eyes close
for a moment...
He is right here in my premise,
isn't He?
Dear friend,
Hold His hand and
bring Him to me.
Rose water made of white petals,
I prepare to
welcome Him.
Dear friend,
Hasn't my letter reached Him?
Or has He betrayed me?
My eyes long
to greet Him.
Take me to His abode.

I spread a crotchet carpet
to lie down,
to write to Him.
I hear His call...
I look all around
in the dense forest.
Dear friend,
He said He would come today.
Then why this waiting?

Dear friend,
please come and
listen to my endless questions...

He has now left the city!
My city!
Dear friend…Your compassion is incomparable.
Do come to apply balm on
my bleeding heart.
Look around…do you see Him?
I have gone blind in His love.
When I see the dark clouds, it is Him there.
When I look out from my window,
at the forest,
it is only Him that I see.
Dear friend,
He has left me immobile.
I hesitate to cross the river without Him.
I refuse to put a morsel of food in my mouth.
I feel Him with me,
every moment of the day,
but I do not see Him…
Why this torture…?
Dear friend

Disentangle

Long locks of hair
with thousands of snakes
entangled,
she walked free and easy
in the op

where the cows with bells tied
around their necks
grazed all day.

She was born
with this boon,
with thousands of snakes,
entangled
into her long curls
of tresses.

Thousands of snakes
moved comfortably and naturally
on her head
as she walked and walked
down the slope of a hill.

Close to the horizon,
she came down to a plain
where the snakes slowly made their way
into her long slender neck
and travelled downwards
to her lean shoulders...
right into her arms and slid
through her thin fingers.

At the horizon,
she took refuge under a tree.
The snakes moved out
to the trunk and down
the branches and crawled
out of her body.

And she fell asleep,
fast asleep
into a dream.

Maya

The music goes on and on

in the background,

as I move to the beat

of His flute.

Slowly and steadily,

holding on to a pleat

of my indigo sari,

with my fingertips,

I danced and danced

till dusk weaved the stars

and the moon,

the sun escaped

into the darkness.

And the moon

was woven completely

into a crescent.

All through this

I cried and wept

and cried and wept,

for I saw Him.

I smiled

while my tears,

dried deep on my face.

Tears are good,

for us to shine.

Let people say whatever.

Tears are good,

for us to shine.

These Plastic Buntings

Two young girls walk past

a pile of plastic garbage.

They look at it, while

their mother takes them,

by their hands

to a nearby street vendor.

She buys some strawberries

in a plastic container,

and grabs her young girls'

hands again.

They walk away.

I wait in my car at a signal light.

Right outside my door

is a pile of plastic garbage.

Young girls with their mother

walk past my car.

The music in my car stereo plays,

the night song,

the empty plastic case of the disc

lies in front,

beside the driver's seat.

I drive away.

People young and old step across,

a pile of plastic garbage,

to enter a restaurant.

A lit-up plastic orange neon sign board reads

'Mast Kalandar'.

They walk in.

Plastic water cups sprawled around,

on the plywood table tops.

A mother grabs hold of her two young girls

and walk past me.

I walk past the primary educated young waiter,

holding a blue plastic tub,

full of plastic.

A pile-full of plastic

with morsels of rice.

Cows gorge on the rice,

with mouth full of plastic.

Little girls walk past,

I wait in my car at a traffic signal.

People young and old step across,

a pile of plastic garbage,

leaving

a bountiful future

of this.

I wake up the next morning.

The Sun is seeping through,

my large glass windows

shining bright.

I open those windows

and step out

to the garden,

where hibiscus

of varied hues grow.

I walk past them,

to slide open

the gates.

A mahogany tree,

has coloured plastic buntings

of political parties,

piled up,

on top of each other,

like paper kites

hung

and left abandoned.

I leap up as high as I can

to reach and tear apart,

these coloured plastic buntings

of political parties

who have already lost

a war,

futile and frivolous.

Acknowledgements

I always wondered about those who wrote poetry with such ease. I would buy poetry books and simply browse through them and go to sleep.

Never in my wildest dreams did I think that one day, I will have a book of poems to my name.

This has happened because of the blessings of my Guru, Sadhguru Jaggi Vasudev. My gratitude to Him.

I would also like to thank Suhaan Mukerji, who patiently heard my poems and encouraged me from start to finish, my sister Rashmi, who supported me when I began writing and Sushma, who gave me honest feedback and helped me to look deeper into my writing, my brother, Harsha, who read and enjoyed my poems.

Rupa Publications, for making this book a reality.

Last but not the least, my friends, Shama, Nitya, Seema and Shaili, for taking out time to read my work.